IMAGES
of America

GROTON

IMAGES
of America

GROTON

Rosemarie Palmer Tucker

ARCADIA
PUBLISHING

Published by Arcadia Publishing
Charleston SC, Chicago IL, Portsmouth NH, San Francisco CA

Library of Congress Control Number: 2008942610

For all general information contact Arcadia Publishing at:
Telephone 843-853-2070
Fax 843-853-0044
E-mail sales@arcadiapublishing.com
For customer service and orders:
Toll-Free 1-888-313-2665

Visit us on the Internet at www.arcadiapublishing.com

*To LaVena Court, Groton Central School history teacher
from 1962 to 1982, who encouraged me to learn history
even when I was not interested.*

CONTENTS

ACKNOWLEDGMENTS

The completion of this book would not have been possible without local residents and organizations sharing their pictures of days past. The Town of Groton Clerk's Office, the Town of Groton Historical Association, Teresa Robinson, Colleen Pierson, Debbie Hubbard, Freda Lucas, and Nancy Senecal Peacock of the Elm Tree Inn contributed pictures. Captions for these pictures are followed by credit for those who shared them. Recognition goes to Paul Duden of Portland, Oregon, who shared the picture of his great-great grandfather Sylvester Pennoyer. If I missed anyone in this listing, please accept my apologies. Unless otherwise noted, images are from the author's collection.

Much research has been done at the Groton Public Library, and I am grateful to Julie Mackey, head library clerk. Gary Lane, Groton resident and owner of Lane's Automotive, assisted by John Oaks of Lansing, New York, identified some of the cars shown in the pictures.

Special thanks to Groton Town Board members Glenn Morey, supervisor; Sheldon Clark; Rick Gamel; Don Scheffler; and Ellard Sovocool for their continued support on my town historian projects. Groton town clerk April Scheffler made a place for me to work in the town building and assisted with the scanning of the cover photograph. I am grateful to her and then deputy town clerk Debbie Lane for our chats about history in our community. Gary Coats, Groton code enforcement officer, shared information for identifying pictures.

Deputy historian for the town of Groton and friend Terry Donlick provided pictures and continued support, traveled with me on research trips, attended conferences, and helped me to interpret some of Groton's history.

My high school history teacher LaVena Court, to whom this book is dedicated, always told me as I struggled to learn history, "You'll get this some day!" When I was appointed historian for the town of Groton in 2001, she remembered back to those school days and said, "I told you that you would get this!" Mrs. Court, I am grateful to you for your teaching and continued friendship.

INTRODUCTION

Settled in the late 1790s, the town of Division was formed on April 7, 1817, from the Cayuga County town of Locke. With its new name of Division, the town became part of Tompkins County on April 17, 1817. On March 13, 1818, community residents successfully petitioned to have the town's name changed to Groton. The town encompasses 50 square miles in northeastern Tompkins County, and the 1820 census reported its population to be 2,803. By 1855, the census reported 3,404. The village of Groton was incorporated in June 1860 and was built on land owned principally by Dea. William Williams. John Perrin and Jonas Williams were early settlers in the village area, with Perrin having built the first log house in 1797. Williams is known to have constructed the first frame structure in 1806.

As a 19th-century industrial center, an early iron foundry within the village brought way for the manufacturing of road rollers, iron truss bridges, steam engines, separators, spoke machines, agricultural implements, and carriages. In 1876, the Groton Carriage Company became an incorporated business, manufacturing carriages, wagons, and cutters. With a statewide demand, the company began large-scale manufacturing, and items became famous throughout the state. Crandall Typewriter Company moved to Groton in 1887 and in the early 1900s became the Standard Typewriter Company. Typewriters with interchangeable type, known as Corona, were manufactured here, and Groton was once known as the "typewriter capital of the world." This typewriter manufacturing company became Smith-Corona Marchant in later years and closed manufacturing in Groton in the 1980s.

Both town and village display a rich architectural legacy. The area includes Greek Revival, Gothic, Italianate, Queen Anne, French Second Empire, and American craftsman–style homes. The town of Groton includes the hamlets of Groton City, McLean, Peruville, and West Groton. Throughout the early years, these hamlets were booming with businesses and industry.

Situated on the Owasco Lake watershed, the town of Groton has rolling hills and valleys. The principal streams are Owasco Inlet and Fall Creek. The town is bisected by New York State Route 38, which runs north–south. North of the Old Peruville Road intersection of New York State Route 38 marks what was once the boundary between the Cayuga and Onondaga Nations (a boundary respected by both). New York State Route 222 enters from the east. The 2000 census reported 5,794 residents of which 2,470 resided within the village.

Throughout its history, Groton has had many good-sized companies that provided an income to its residents as well as products that were sold locally, nationally, and internationally. As time made changes and changes gave rise to new needs in the community, the nation, and the world, the businesses of Groton advanced with the times. Today with Smith-Corona Marchant having closed its doors after 70 years of business in Groton, there is now a new company, Plastisol. Plastisol puts together premade bodies of fire trucks.

The community is proud of the many historical facts, businesses, and people associated with the town and village. Benn Conger, born in 1856, was a member of the New York State Assembly from 1900 to 1901, a member of the New York State Senate (41st district) from 1909 to 1910; and an entrepreneur investing in many businesses of the area. He built his large "mansion on the hill," which today houses the Benn Conger Inn. Dexter Hubbard Marsh, born in 1840 in Groton, was cofounder of the First National Bank of Groton and served as its first cashier and its second president. He personally invested in many new businesses in Groton, such as the Crandall Typewriter Company, the Groton Carriage Company, N. R. Streeter and Company, as well as promoting and organizing the Southern Central Railroad through Groton. His wife, Welthea (Backus) Marsh, born in 1841 in Groton, became the first and only woman president of the First National Bank of Groton (1896 to 1901). She was also a director and president of the Crandall Typewriter Company and director and treasurer of the Groton Carriage Company. Nelson R. Streeter, inventor of mousetraps, sad irons, trivets for irons, tri-fold mirrors that are found in clothing stores, and may other items, lived in Groton many years and was founder and owner of N. R. Streeter Company. He was also a poet and published "Gems from an Old Drummer's Grip" in 1889. Charles Perrigo, cofounder and first president of the First National Bank of Groton, was co-owner of the company that manufactured steam traction engines and the Separator (both made in Groton).

The 1914 *American Agriculturist Farm Directory* lists businesses in Groton, including A. J. McMahon's on Cortland Street, for sales of farm implements and wagons; Allen and Stoddard on Spring Street, for coal, lumber, hay, and grain; F. J. Heywood on Spring Street, for blacksmithing and general repair; veterinarian G. G. Stevens on Cayuga Street; and Standard Typewriter Company, with Benn Conger as president, on the corner of Spring and Main Streets. Liveries included A. J. Metzgar on Cayuga Street, H. C. Sandvich on Main Street, and B. H. Main on Main Street. The Groton Bridge Company, with Jay Conger as president, is listed on Main Street; James Taylor had a bowling alley on Cortland Street; and M. A. Murray had the Groton five-and-ten cent store on Cortland Street. The First National Bank of Groton, with G. M. Stoddard as president, and the Mechanics Bank, with Benn Conger as president, were both located on Main Street. As time passed, business were lost to floods, fires, or just torn down.

Groton includes pictures of houses, businesses, churches, schools, and other buildings, some no longer here and others that still exist. There are also pictures of the demolitions of businesses and manufacturing companies. A section on people includes those who have invested financially, religiously, academically, and as longtime families in the community.

One

VILLAGE SCENES

Once known as Groton Hollow, the village of Groton was incorporated in June 1860 and is located in the center of the town of Groton. Shown on this 1866 map are the names of the businesses, churches, and property owners. Street names and the location of school district No. 8 and two cemeteries are also indicated.

The photographer took this picture looking northeast into the village. Since the Smith Corona typewriter factory is not seen here, the picture is dated before 1916, possibly the late 1890s. The white building just above "Bird's" in the title is where the museum of the Town of Groton Historical Association is located today.

Located on the southeast corner of Main and Cortland Streets, construction began on this building in 1853. Lumber was cut from a forest on nearby Salt Road. Called Hotel Goodyear in this 1908 photograph, the building is currently known as the Groton Hotel.

The Groton Opera House was located just east of Hotel Goodyear. Three companies of the Groton Fire Department kept their fire wagons and equipment in the ground-level area. The performing area was on the second floor. The structure later became a movie theater.

This view from the late 1800s or early 1900s is from Mill Street, now West Cortland Street, looking at the bandstand that once stood in the middle of the four corners. Such a structure could not exist today, with cars and trucks on the road. Main Street goes to the right, Cortland Street is straight from the photographer, and Cayuga Street is to the left. (Courtesy of the Town of Groton Historical Association.)

This view of Main Street is looking north from the Harris house towards the four corners of Main, Cayuga, Cortland, and Mill Streets. The photograph is from late 1890s or early 1900s. (Courtesy of the Town of Groton Historical Association.)

This view of Main Street is looking south. The Harris house is shown on the right. It is now the museum for the Town of Groton Historical Association. Notice the dirt road. The item located at the foot of the tree was used to step down from carriages. (Courtesy of the Town of Groton Historical Association.)

Another Main Street view looking south shows a wagon pulled by two horses. Behind the wagon is a carriage being pulled by a horse that is wearing a straw hat on its head. Notice the wooden sidewalk, allowing pedestrians to cross the dirt road. (Courtesy of the History Center in Tompkins County.)

Here a band marches on Cortland Street. The opera house is the white four-story building on the left. Notice the sign, which reads, "The Atwood Stables Hitching & Feeding." The stables and livery are actually in the building partially hidden to the left of the sign. Manley Gale and Lynn Carrington, born in 1896 and 1893, respectively, are the young boys walking on the sidewalk. (Courtesy of the Town of Groton Historical Association.)

This band is standing in front of the opera house, which is also home to three companies of the Groton Fire Department. (Courtesy of the Town of Groton Historical Association.)

Volunteer members of the Citizens Hook and Ladder Company show their ladder cart to children. The names over the doors of the building indicate which fire company houses equipment in the ground level of the Groton Opera House. From left to right, they are Pioneer Hose Company No. 1, Conger Hose Company No. 2, and Citizens Hook and Ladder Company No. 3. (Courtesy of the Town of Groton Historical Association.)

Here is Cortland Street looking west. It appears to be a busy day on this street. There are men with horses and wagons willing to stop to have their picture taken. The bandstand is shown in the center of the four corners. (Courtesy of the Town of Groton Historical Association.)

This picture of Main Street looks south. The large white building on the left is the F. C. Atwood Store and Hotel. That building and the large one on the right no longer exist. They each have been replaced with parking lots.

This is a view of South Main Street. The houses shown in this picture still exist. Notice the wooden sidewalk crossing the dirt road. On the right side is St. Anthony's Catholic Church, the taller brick building with the peaked roof.

In 1867, Corydon Conger was contracted to build a railroad through the village for the Southern Central Railroad. Completed in 1869, the town paid $50,000, and stock was sold to raise another $50,000 from the citizens for its construction. The Southern Central later became the Lehigh Valley Railroad. Train traffic in Groton ended in 1978. This view looks north.

Although windows are boarded up, doors are locked, and the building needs paint, the railroad depot still exists today. However, the tracks have been removed, and the water tower is no longer there. This view looks south.

Rail was once a popular way to travel to places beyond Groton. The conductor is Dan Stiles. The man in the suit is Groton's Dr. George E. Albon, with his daughter Marjorie. Albon is seen here after going to Auburn to call on a patient. He was born in England about 1865. Marjorie was also born in England about 1904.

PICTURESQUE
LEHIGH VALLEY
RAILROAD

"Anthracite Coal used exclusively, insuring Cleanliness and Comfort."

Time Table.
IN EFFECT MAY, 17, 1895.

Auburn - Division.

SOUTHWARD.

STATION	A M 10	A M 112	A M 4	A M †42	6	6
N F Have	....	....	....	....	5 02	....
Sterling	....	....	....	....	5 20	....
Cato	....	....	....	....	5 28	....
Woodsport	....	....	....	....	6 11	....
Auburn	12 5	8 16	*9 10	11 15	6 45	*6 45
Moravia	1 8	8 52	9 54	12 45	7 22	7 22
Locke	31 26	8 58	10 10	12 45	7 29	7 29
GROTON	1 40	9 10	10 2	1 25	7 42	7 42
Freeville	2 3	9 20	10 20	2 05	7 54	7 54
Dryden	2 9	9 2	10 54	2 25	8 00	8 00
Berkshire	2 33	9 58	11 33	3 45	8 33	8 33
Newark Val	2 48	10 10	11 41	4 10	8 45	8 45
Owego	3 01	10 30	12 12	5 00	9 05	9 05
Sayre	4 30	11 00	12 55	5 20	9 41	9 40

NORTHWARD.

STATIONS.	A M 5	A M 133	A M 201	P M 1	P M 9	A M 5
Sayre	5 15	7 10	8 15	*4 25	6 30	*5 50
Owego	6 14	8 25	9 40	5 08	6 54	6 25
Newark Val	6 28	8 52	10 44	5 52	7 13	6 44
Berkshire	6 37	8 43	11 33	6 6	7 24	6 56
Dryden	7 05	9 14	1 16	6 30	7 48	7 25
Freeville	7 09	9 20	1 20	6 40	7 50	7 35
GROTON	7 18	9 31	2 15	6 55	8 05	7 46
Locke	7 25	9 42	2 40	7 6	8 15	7 15
Moravia	7 31	9 48	2 55	7 21	8 21	8 02
Auburn	8 20	10 30	3 55	8 10	9 00	8 43
Woodsport	8 48	10 52	..	....	....	....
Cato	9 08	11 06	..	....	....	....
Sterling	9 25	11 37	..	....	....	....
N.F. Haven	9 53	11 30	..	....	....	....

* Trains run daily.
† Sunday train only.
‡ Stops on signal.
All other trains daily, except Sunday.

CONNECTIONS
Owego with N.Y., L. E. & W. R. R.; Freeville with E. C. & N. R. R.; Auburn with N. Y., C. & H R. R.; Woodsport with N. Y., C. & H. R. R., and West Shore R. R.; Sterling with R. W. & O. R. R

A. W. NONNEMACHER, Ass't Gen'l Pass'er Agt., South Bethlehem, Pa.
CHAS. S. LEE, General Passenger Agent, Philadelphia, Pa.
ROLLIN H. WILBUR, General Supt., South Bethlehem, Pa.

This 1895 schedule shows the times of arrivals and departures for Groton. One could travel to places as near as Locke or Freeville, each four miles away, or as far as Sayre, Pennsylvania, which probably took a little less than an hour and a half.

A busy day at the Groton depot could mean there was an event going on in town. Labeled on the railroad car across the upper edge is "Lehigh Valley Railroad." Along the side and below the window is written, "United States of America Railroad Post Office."

18

In 1914, a bandstand was located on Main Street. The school shown in the background fronts on Church Street, with the back side facing Main Street.

This winter scene is of Main Street, and the viewer is looking north. The white house with the shutters located on the right was once the home of Harry and Ione Masters. This house and others shown no longer exist.

The Groton Telephone Office is the brick building on the right. It was located on the southwest corner of Railroad and Main Streets. Paul McMahon's garage is the two-story white building. The corner of Lincoln Avenue is shown on the left. The garage and telephone office burned in the early 1960s, along with other buildings on Railroad Street.

Digging up the dirt road near the four corners of Main, Cortland, Cayuga, and Mill Streets requires many men, since it was all hand labor. These men are preparing the road for the laying of bricks to bring the road up to date for the times.

The bricks have been delivered and are awaiting installation into the newly smoothed dirt road. The work required many people to get the job done. A passerby takes a quick look at the photographer.

The northeast corner of Main and Cayuga Streets was known as the Baldwin Block. Businesses in the building include the Groton Chamber of Commerce, Top Hat Billiards, Dunlap's Furniture, a market, and the Spa, which was a candy and lunch counter. The building on the far right with the peaked roof is a hardware store. The car on the left is a 1935 or 1936 Ford. The truck is a 1928 or 1929 Ford.

The building that was originally the opera house became the Corona Theater. Fire trucks were housed through the entrance to the right of the front doorway. On the right side of the marquee is a playbill advertising the 1939 movie *Gone with the Wind*. The car on the left is a 1933 or 1934 Chrysler.

22

The Goodyear Memorial Library is a public library. In his will, Dr. Miles Goodyear requested that a public library be built to honor his mother, Elizabeth Goodyear. Ithaca architect William Henry Miller designed this Adam colonial-style brick structure. Construction began in 1916 and was completed in 1917 at a cost of $20,000. The dedication was held on Friday, July 13, 1917.

This is the interior of the Goodyear Memorial Library. Located on Cortland Street, the library looks much like this today. The iron frames for the windows were ordered from England. The furniture was manufactured by H. H. Bool Company of Ithaca. Visitors to the library will see that the tables, chairs, librarian's desk, bookshelves, and lamps are still utilized in this wonderful reading room. The photograph was taken about 1917.

This gentleman is showing off his 1928 Hudson to a friend. Joseph L. Hudson, a Detroit entrepreneur and founder of Hudson's department store, provided the capital and gave permission for the Hudson Motor Car Company to use his name. Sales of the Hudson began in 1909. The cost of one car was $1,000. The Hudson was manufactured in Detroit until 1954.

The Metro-Goldwyn-Mayer (MGM) train came to Groton, as shown in this photograph. The reason for the visit is unknown. It is believed it may be to promote a new movie being shown in town.

The picture is looking at Williams Street towards the corner of Cortland Street. The brick house on the right belonged to Jennie Conant Conger, the wife of Frank Conger, and still exists. Notice the people having a conversation on the sidewalk on the left. (Courtesy of the Town of Groton Historical Association.)

This view of Cortland Street looking south on Church Street shows a fountain in the middle of the road and a wooden sidewalk. The houses shown in this picture still exists today.

This view of Church Street is from in front of the Congregational church looking north towards Cortland Street.

This picture shows what is referred to as the old swimming hole. Although children used the creeks near their homes for swimming, this one may be the creek running along Cayuga Street. (Courtesy of Terry Donlick.)

Old Home Days have been held in Groton since 1934. This shows the activity during sidewalk sales. The shop known as the Market Basket, located across the street, was a business that occupied different storefronts throughout its years. (Courtesy of the History Center in Tompkins County.)

This picture of Main Street looking south shows the Corona Typewriter Company's smokestack. It was probably taken on a busy Saturday in the late 1930s or early 1940s. Notice that some cars parked parallel to the curb and others parked diagonal. The first car on the right is a Chrysler from the 1930s.

The Owasco Inlet runs through the village west of Main Street, and there were times when flooding occurred. This July 1935 flood picture was taken in front of the Tavern, which was located on Main Street just north of the telephone office. (Courtesy of the Groton Town Historian archives.)

This picture shows the July 1935 flood in front of Paul McMahon's garage. This building was located on Main Street where Walter's car dealership is today. The building burned in 1963. (Courtesy of the Groton Town Historian archives.)

This demonstrates a safe way to get across the flooded area, by tying a rope from a house to another building, hooking up a washtub to a rope and pulley, and riding above the waters. The photograph was taken in July 1935. The following picture shows that his destination is the awaiting fire truck. (Courtesy of the Groton Town Historian archives.)

Shown in this Cayuga Street picture are the guardrail cables that are located between the street and the creek. Visible is the rope used to bring people across the creek and the roadway to the awaiting fire truck during the July 1935 flood. The fire truck is the destination of the person riding across the water in the previous picture. (Courtesy of the Groton Town Historian archives.)

This photograph was probably taken during the 1960 village of Groton centennial celebration. The Grand Union building is now the site of Walpole's Variety, Walpole's Liquor Store, and Walpole's Real Estate Office. The building to its right and the houses were removed for the construction of the current building of the First National Bank of Groton. Loretta's Shear Excellence is now located in the two-story building to the left of the Grand Union. (Courtesy of the Town of Groton Historical Association.)

This July 1963 picture shows the buildings that were once part of the Baldwin Block. They were demolished to make room for the new Groton Post Office building.

This is a July 1963 view of the west side of the Baldwin Block before the demolition. Trucks are ready and waiting for large equipment to arrive.

In July 1963, equipment removed a large portion of the Baldwin Block; only the smaller building remains in this picture.

The Smith Corona Company, manufacturer of typewriters, constructed this building in 1916. This 1984 picture was taken just before demolition of the factory. The company previously employed hundreds of people for 70 years.

This is a view of the back side of the Smith Corona factory at the time of its demolition in 1984.

As more and more of this four-story typewriter factory was demolished in 1984, a part of Groton's history went with it. Bricks were sold for $1 each, and the proceeds went to benefit the Town of Groton Historical Association.

This 1984 picture shows the south side of the typewriter factory. It is almost gone. As times passed and community members became involved, opportunities arose for Groton to continue to plan and work towards its future.

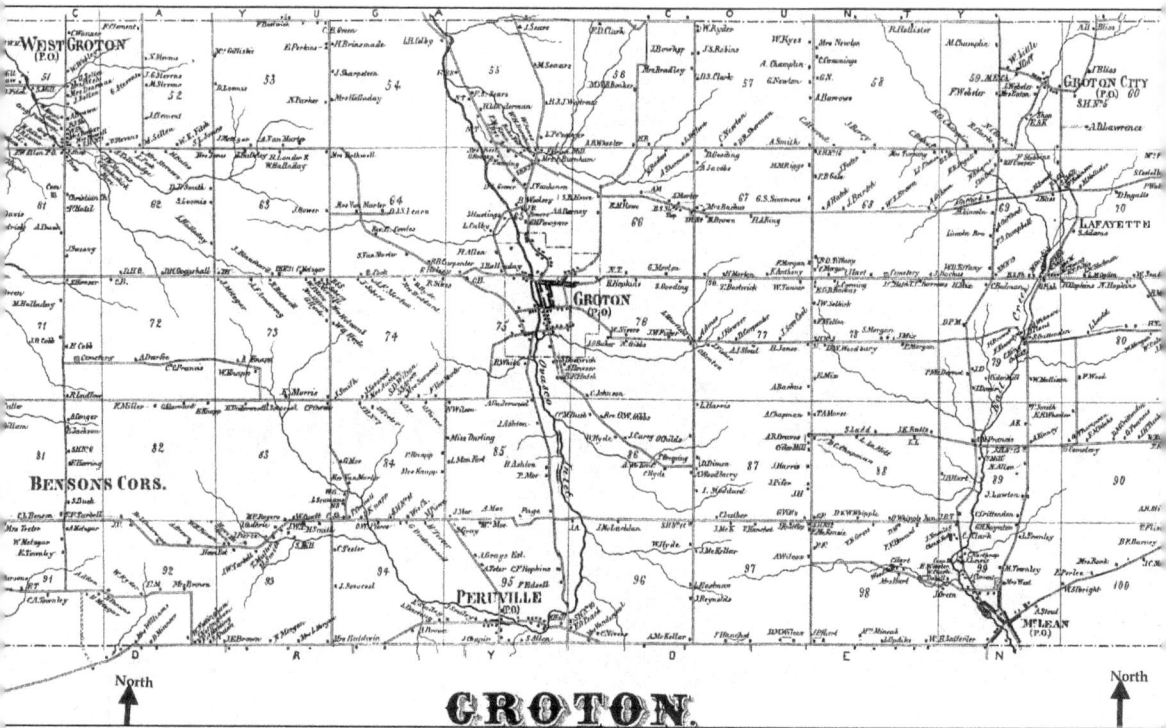

North   North

GROTON.

An 1866 map of the town of Groton is shown here. At 5 miles wide and 10 miles long, Groton is bordered on the north by Cayuga County's town of Locke, on the east by Cortland County, and on the south and west by the Tompkins County towns of Dryden and Lansing, respectively. Lots numbered 51 to 100 were assigned as part of the military tract following the Revolutionary War. Looking closely, one can see names of property owners and businesses and the location of churches, cemeteries, and school districts.

34

Two

HAMLETS

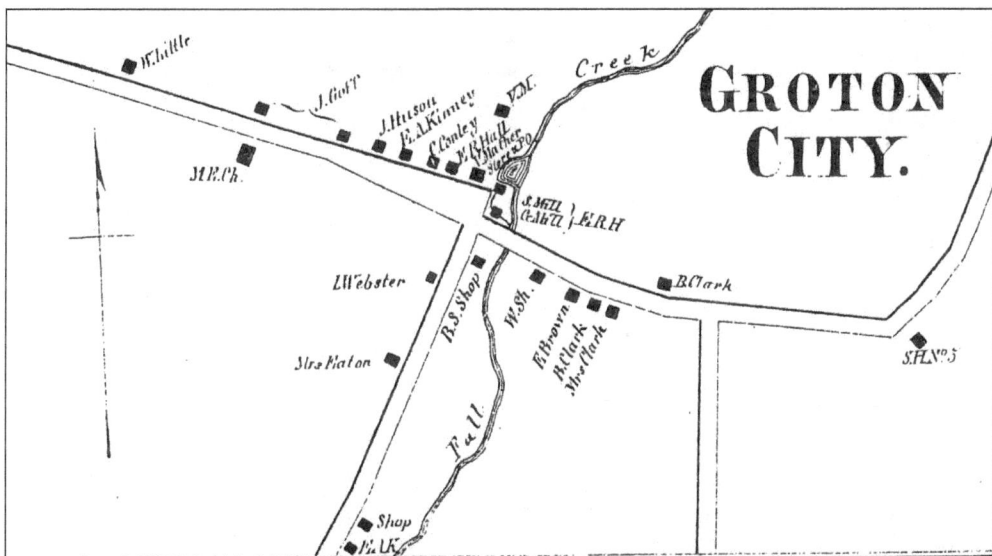

This 1866 map of the hamlet of Groton City indicates the businesses that were once active in the area. Named Groton City, it was hoped that this area would become the main area of the town. When the railroad came through in the late 1860s, the village area became the most active with business and the buildings of homes and churches. This chapter will provide pictures of the hamlets of Groton, including Groton City, Peruville, McLean, and West Groton. During the early years, these hamlets were once booming with businesses, industry, post offices, mills, schools, and churches.

This picture of Groton City shows a wood fence to keep farm animals out of the road. More pictures of Groton City can be found in chapter 3. (Courtesy of the Town of Groton Historical Association.)

This picture shows the bridge in Groton City. Manufactured by the Groton Bridge Company, it still exists at this location. (Courtesy of the Town of Groton Historical Association.)

The general store in Groton City was once owned by Milo Gillen. Jay Thomas purchased it from Gillen in 1902. The store closed in the 1940s after serving the community for over 150 years. Ike Sobers made rural deliveries for this store using his gray horse and buggy and a cutter in the winter. (Courtesy of the Town of Groton Historical Association.)

This Groton City sawmill picture is dated 1910. Groton City was a lumbering community with numerous sawmills and was once known as "Slab City" due the quantity of lumber found at the mills. There were many other businesses in the area. Once the train began through the village of Groton, business became more prominent in the village and Groton City became more of a farming area. (Courtesy of the Town of Groton Historical Association.)

A Groton City mill and box factory are shown in this 1910 picture. Other businesses in this area were a cider mill, a cheese factory, a creamery, gristmills, a cloth mill, and a post office. At one time, Groton City did more business than Groton Hollow, the area that became the village of Groton. (Courtesy of the Town of Groton Historical Association.)

This 1866 map of Peruville indicates the businesses that were once an active part of this hamlet, located in the southern part of the town. Peruville borders Dryden and Lansing.

This is a picture of the mill that was once an active business in Peruville. (Courtesy of the Town of Groton Historical Association.)

Peruville's blacksmith shop was a busy place when a horse needed shoeing and carriages and wagons needed repair. (Courtesy of the Town of Groton Historical Association.)

This 1976 picture shows what was once the community center in the hamlet of Peruville. Many community meetings, dances, and other gatherings took place here. It later became a residence. (Courtesy of the Groton Town Clerk's archives.)

This 1866 map of the hamlet of McLean indicates the density of the hamlet. Although the post offices in the other hamlets closed in the early 1900s, McLean still has its own post office and zip code. More pictures of McLean can be found in chapter 3.

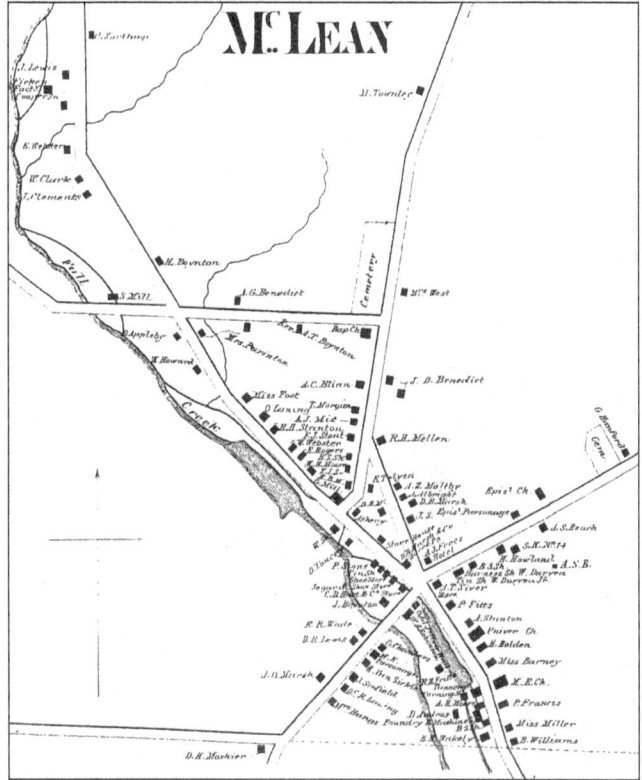

Amasa Cobb arrived in the McLean area about 1796 and built the first log cabin and the first tavern on the site of the Elm Tree Inn. The tree pictured in this 1940s photograph was just a forest sapling at that time. (Courtesy of Nancy Senecal Peacock.)

Fred H. Maricle, born in 1866, owned this general store in the late 1890s and early 1900s in the hamlet of McLean. This picture shows his delivery wagon and team ready to make deliveries. (Courtesy of Nancy Senecal Peacock.)

This building was constructed in 1824 to replace an earlier one that burned. In the 1870s, Daniel B. Marsh owned the store. As shown in the previous picture, Maricle later owned the business. Although currently empty, the building still exists today and is located where Stevens Road and Church Street come together in McLean. (Courtesy of Nancy Senecal Peacock.)

L. H. Dunham of McLean owned and trained oxen. This 1939 picture shows him with Tom and Jerry, his red Devon oxen. He showed his trained oxen at county fairs, Fourth of July celebrations, and Old Home Days events. Born about 1870, his interest in oxen began when he was nine years old. The printing was added to the photograph and was not actually on the wagon. (Courtesy of Nancy Senecal Peacock.)

The barrel factory in McLean is long gone but was a very active business at one time. (Courtesy of Nancy Senecal Peacock.)

The McLean Creamery no longer exists but was a very important business for the rural areas of Groton and McLean. (Courtesy of Nancy Senecal Peacock.)

Here is Fred H. Maricle in June 1910 with his team and grocery wagon ready to go into the country to deliver merchandise. There was a post office located in this store. The houses on the left side no longer exist, and the site is now home of the McLean Fire Department.

PATRONS OF HUSBANDRY.

National Grange Incorporated January, 1873.

Deputies organizing Granges are requested to send a copy of this sheet to the Secretary of their State Grange at the same time they send the application and fee to Tippecanoe City, Ohio.

To C. M. FREEMAN, *Secretary of National Grange,*

Tippecanoe City, Ohio.

The undersigned have organized a Subordinate Grange in the

Town of *McLean*, County of *Tompkins*

State of *New York*, *and most respectfully ask for a Dispensation and*

all necessary documents and enclose the fee of Fifteen Dollars for the same.

NAMES OF APPLICANTS.

D. R. Stout, Mrs. D. R. Stout, George B. McKinney, D. W. Rowle
Andrew Steele, Mrs. Andrew Steele, Miss Minnie Steele,
A. F. Howard, Henry McKee, Mrs. Henry McKee,
G. B. French, Hugh Foster, D. H. Hoffman,
F. E. Trapp, F. H. Benedict, Mrs. F. H. Benedict,
Miss Freda L. Benedict, R. S. Steadman,

Mrs. R. D. Stout, *Lecturer.*
P. O. Address
McLean N.Y.

F. E. Trapp, *Master.*   F. H. Benedict, *Secretary.*
P. O. Address   P. O. Address
McLean N.Y.   McLean N.Y.

Nearest Express Office McLean, *County of* Tompkins

Name of Grange McLean Grange.   1075

Organized and approved by Cantine Lounsbery

Date, Nov 20 06   *P. O. Address* Brookton

Tompkins Co. N.Y.

INSTRUCTIONS TO DEPUTIES.

The Grange organized will receive all necessary documents with their dispensation, and in the meantime can be appointing their committees, preparing their hall, and balloting for candidates. Dispensations will invariably be sent within forty-eight hours after the receipt of the application. Write additional names on back.

Incorporated in 1873, the National Grange was primarily an organization for small, rural communities, and it began as an agricultural organization. Cantine Lounsbery of Brookton approved McLean's Grange No. 1075 on November 20, 1906. The document includes many McLean names. (Courtesy of Nancy Senecal Peacock.)

This 1866 map of the hamlet of West Groton shows the main four corners where businesses thrived.

Records for this general store go back to 1812, including those of first owner, J. L. Brinkerhoff. In 1916, Frank E. Pierson purchased it and announced that he would operate solely for the benefit of this farming and dairying community. Located near the busy four corners of West Groton Road and Cobb Street, the store continued with the Pierson family for many years. (Courtesy of the Groton Town Clerk's archives.)

This is a sales card for Pierson's store, dated 1933. The cost of similar items today makes for an interesting comparison. (Courtesy of Colleen Pierson.)

1933

These Prices Good At

PIERSON'S STORE
West Groton

for the balance of the year unless sold out before

10 lbs. Granulated Sugar 50c
2 lb. box Soda Crackers 19c
Post Bran or Farina .... pkg. 10c
Ralston Wheat Cereal 22c
Mixed Nuts. .....lb. 21c   Walnuts, small 20c
        Extra fancy white meats ..... 28c lb.
Chocolate Creams or Gum Drops .... 10c lb.
Fancy Ribbon Candy .... 18c lb.
South American Popcorn .... 2 lbs. 25c
        It sure does pop
2 lbs. Jumbo Green Peanuts 25c
Pineapple Florida Oranges, 23c doz,   2 doz. 45c
Tidex Medium Motor Oil .... 2 gal. cans 95c
Radiator Alcohol .... 55c gal.
Oneida Jump Traps .... $1.25 doz.
        Less than mail order prices
McKay Tire Chains .... $3.98 set
        Out wear 2 or 3 sets of cheap ones
Coontail Felt Boots .... $2.00 pr.
Men's All Wool Socks .... 35c pr.
Boys' Sheep Lined Coats .... $2.99 up
Mayflower Flour $1.19
        money back if not entirely satisfactory
        You will find it as good as any on the market
N. Y. State Rich, Full Milk Cheese .... 19c lb.
Lettuce Leaf Salad Dressing .... Qt. cans 25c
2 lb. Jars Peanut Butter 30c

Frank C. Pierson.

Pierson is seen here with his delivery wagon and team setting up for selling his merchandise. The umbrella advertises Buttrick and Frawley, a clothing store in Ithaca. (Courtesy of Colleen Pierson.)

From 1845 to 1860, West Groton was a thriving community. Some of the businesses at that time included two stores, a wagon shop, a tannery, a carpet-weaving shop, two cooper shops, two shoe shops, three blacksmith shops, and a tavern. The barn shown in this picture was once a tavern and was located on the corner of West Groton Road and Cobb Street. (Courtesy of Colleen Pierson.)

SOCIAL PARTY,

Yourself and lady are cordially invited to attend a Social Party to be held at the

NEW PUBLIC HALL, WEST GROTON, N. Y.

Friday Evening, August 14th, 1891,

MUSIC BY SHAVER'S ORCHESTRA,

Dancing 50 cents,

Supper & Horse Extra,

By order com.

There was once a public hall in the hamlet of West Groton. Those living in the community could purchase stock and become owners of the facility. Many community events took place, including a social party, as advertised on this 1891 card.

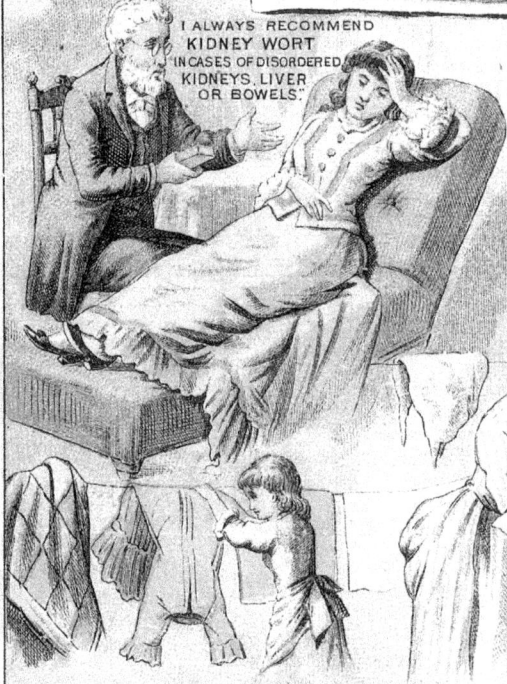

The 1884 *New York State Almanac* carried many advertisements. Anson B. Rogers, a previous owner of the Pierson store, advertised on its back cover, which would have cost more than advertising inside. The front cover of the almanac had a picture of New York State governor Grover Cleveland. (Courtesy of Colleen Pierson.)

Three

SCHOOLS AND CHURCHES

While the town of Groton was still part of Cayuga County and the town of Locke, the first school was built of logs in 1815 on one-quarter of an acre and became district No. 1. This 1915 picture was taken when West Groton celebrated the centennial of the district. The original log structure was replaced in 1856 by the building shown here. Today it is a private residence. (Courtesy of Colleen Pierson.)

District No. 1 teacher Ellie A. L. Bulkley is shown in this 1915 picture. Although it was common for married women to not teach, the 1920 and 1930 censuses listed her as a teacher. Married to William H. Bulkley, she was also the librarian responsible for more than 650 books. (Courtesy of Colleen Pierson.)

Groton citizens raised funds to build the Groton Academy on Church Street in 1838. Known throughout the state for over 30 years, the 1839 enrollment shows 206 pupils from seven states. Tuition was $4 to $10 per term, depending on the department, and there were three terms to a school year. Weekly room and board in the village ranged from $1.25 to $1.50. Fire took the structure in 1882.

CERTIFICATE OF ACADEMIC SCHOLARSHIP.

Groton Academy.

This is to Certify, *That H. G. Moe is a member of Groton Academy, and that at an examination held this day, he has been found to have attained the proficiency required by the ordinance of the Regents of the University, to entitle him to be classed as an Academic scholar in any Academy subject to the visitation of the Regents.*

S. Hopkins
H. Bowker ⎬ *Committee.*

M. M. Baldwin *Principal.*

Dated Nov 22 1865.

This November 1865 certificate was received by Hiram G. Moe for his completion of studies at the Groton Academy. Moe became a clerk at the First National Bank of Groton. Signatures include principal M. M. Baldwin, S. Hopkins, and H. Bowker.

District No. 12 was known as the Fitts School and was located on the southwest corner of Salt and Stevens Roads. It combined with other Groton schools, becoming centralized before 1931.

District No. 4 was known as the Morton School and was located on the southwest corner of Lick Street and what is now Old Stage Road. (Courtesy of the Town of Groton Historical Association.)

These children are arriving for their day at the Morton School. Notice the lunch containers carried by the last two children. The first two girls are pulling a young child on a sled. To the right is the school's flagpole. (Courtesy of the History Center in Tompkins County.)

Constructed in 1866 to replace a small building, the Jones Schoolhouse was located on the southeast corner of Elm Street Extension and Salt Road. The district No. 9 building closed in 1943 and was later used by the Groton Grange until the 1970s. This 18-by-23-foot building was sold to a private owner in 2003 and is used for storing farm supplies. (Courtesy of the Town of Groton Historical Association.)

A 1907 picture shows recess at the Jones Schoolhouse. The person in front is Lottie Stevens. Those in line from left to right are Mary Davis, Helen Court, Howard Morgan, Clifford Ranney, Jay Van Burger, Helen Chapman, two unidentified, Mary Stickles, Hattie Stevens, unidentified, Kenneth Ranney, and Harold Fuller. (Courtesy of the Town of Groton Historical Association.)

District No. 11 was located on Spring Street Extension and was known as the Metzgar School. This picture shows a group of students and their teacher. In the fall of 1931, Charlotte Buckingham taught at this school. There are 18 one-room schools indicted on the 1866 map shown on page 34.

The girl standing before the class reciting her lessons is at the Metzgar School. (Courtesy of the History Center in Tompkins County.)

This school in McLean is district No. 20, located on what is now the Cortland-McLean Road. The building was just east of the Elm Tree Inn on the south side of the road. (Courtesy of the History Center in Tompkins County.)

This group of children attended McLean's district No. 20 school. The teacher is Katherine Byrnes. Seen here are, from left to right, (first row) Ora Parmer, Willie McCarthy, Harry Sherwood, Orilla Newcomb, and Lewis Sherwood; (second row) Robert McKinney, Henry Steele, Margaret Steele, Mary Steele, L. A. Lewis, Ethel Stanton, Emma O'Byrne, Ruth Davis, Beatrice Benham, and Jessis Adams; (third row) Gilbert Francis, Carl McKinney, Arthur Lewis, Fred Carter, Hilda Adams, Eugene West, Wells Ducher, George Scofield, Arthur Parmer, DeLos Robins, and Veda Dutcher. Teacher Katherine Byrnes is seen in the back. (Courtesy of the History Center in Tompkins County.)

McLean's district No. 20 schoolhouse is shown in 1955 as an abandoned building. (Courtesy of the History Center in Tompkins County.)

Located on what is now New York State Route 38 south of the village of Groton, district No. 10 was the Peruville School. This group stepped outside for a quick picture. Notice the bike at the left corner of the schoolhouse. Today the building is a private residence. (Courtesy of the Town of Groton Historical Association.)

After the 1882 loss of the Groton Academy to fire, this two-story Groton Union School building was constructed on the Church Street site at a cost of $8,000. It was soon outgrown, and an addition was completed in 1893, making it a three-story structure. The cost for the addition was $9,000. (Courtesy of the Town of Groton Historical Association.)

Here is a group of students enjoying the outdoors. Notice the group to the right standing near the tree. They appear to be dressed up for Halloween or maybe a school play. One young man wears a long white beard. (Courtesy of the Groton Central School District Office.)

These first, second, and third graders are in front of the Groton Union School, which was located on Church Street. The photograph is from about 1905. It is always interesting to see the clothing and hairstyles.

Fourth- and fifth-grade students stand in front of Groton Union School. The photograph is from about 1905.

Seventh- and eighth-grade students stand in front of Groton Union School. The photograph is from about 1905.

High school girls are pictured in front of Groton Union School. The photograph is from about 1905.

High school boys are pictured in front of Groton Union School. Notice that four of the boys are wearing knickers. Evidently the younger high school–age boys still wore knickers and advanced to longer pants at a certain age. The photograph is from about 1905.

This 1921 classical revival high school building became the elementary school in 1954. In 1962, the Smith Corona Typewriter Company used this building for offices. In 1968, it became Tompkins-Cortland Community College, which relocated to its current Dryden location in 1974. Now used for senior housing, Schoolhouse Gardens Apartments was added to the National Register of Historical Places in 1992. Notice the former high school building behind to the right.

The high school on Main Street was completed in 1921 and opened that May. This is the first class to graduate from the new school. Identified in the first row on the far left is Nellie English.

The Groton Opera House was often used for school events; graduations and plays often took place there. This 1935 photograph by Floyd Miller of Miller Studio shows a school play. Notice the person lying across the front of the group dressed as a goat.

In August 1935, boys who were senior agriculture students at Groton School took a trip to Johnson City, New York, to tour the Endicott Johnson Shoe factory. From left to right are (first row) unidentified, Leslie Dorr, John Kocis, Robert Babcock, Frank Scheffler, and Russell Benson; (second row) Clifford Ostrander, Carlton Knapp, teacher Bradley Gormel, Edward Rote, Carroll Champlain, and Stanley Hall.

Groundbreaking for this junior-senior high school building took place on June 4, 1953. Located on Peru Road, it included grades 5 through 12. The building opened in 1954, and the former high school building on Main Street became the elementary school for grades kindergarten through four. This picture was taken in the late 1960s or early 1970s. It was always said that the school was built on quicksand, but it is still there.

The elementary school building on Elm Street was completed in 1962, and the first kindergarten class started there in 1963. The building is very active today with grades kindergarten through fifth. (Courtesy of Teresa Robinson.)

The Methodist Episcopal Society was incorporated in 1836 by the Reverend L. K. Redington and Justus Pennoyer. Their first church building, located on the west side of Church Street, was completed and dedicated in 1842. Following the merging of the Methodist, Congregational, and Baptist Churches in the 1960s, the Groton Fire Department burned this building as a practice. The pastor's home to the left of the church is now a private residence.

First Baptist Church, Groton, N. Y.

Built in 1870 with seating for 600, the Baptist church is located on the corner of Cortland and Church Streets. The Romanesque Revival–style building, popular for post-Civil War Baptist and Methodist churches, was designed by architect Archimedes Russell of Syracuse. The corbelled brickwork is angled with stone trim. Notice the triple-arched entrance and the windows above. The slate roof is gray and lavender.

Designed by architect Lawrence B. Valk of New York City, this high Victorian Gothic–style building was constructed in the 1880s as the Congregational church. The building shown in this picture has a multicolored decorative scheme using brick and fine-glass windows. Dedicated in January 1851, the church had seating for about 300 people. Located on Church Street, it is now privately owned and houses two businesses and a private residence.

St. Anthony's Catholic Church, organized in 1870 by the Reverend Father Gilbert of Ithaca, purchased one acre of land on South Main Street in 1872 at a cost of $400. Construction began on the church in 1873 and was completed in 1874 at a cost of $3,000. Dedicated in October 1874, the building was razed in the late 1970s following construction of a new parish on New York State Route 38 north of the village.

Located at 108 Elm Street, this building was originally constructed as St. Ambrose Episcopal Church. William Henry Miller, who studied architecture at Cornell University, designed this structure. Today it houses the Heritage Baptist Church. (Courtesy of Dewey Dawson.)

In December 1816, a group gathered at Ichabod Brown's home and formed the West Church of Locke. Meetings were held in the homes of members and the schoolhouse until 1833, when the church building was completed at a cost of $500. A steeple was added in 1884. Formerly known as the West Groton Congregational Church, it is currently called the West Groton Bible Church and located on Cobb Street.

The Wesleyan Methodist denomination was formed in 1843 by secession from the Methodist Episcopal Church of Peruville. This building was constructed in 1850 with two doors at the front. It had two aisles and seating for 150 people. The steeple and weather vane that were added in 1879 are not shown in this picture. Originally located on Pleasant Valley Road, it no longer stands today. (Courtesy of the Groton Town Clerk's archives.)

Located on Groton City Road in Groton City, it is believed that the Groton City United Church of Christ was once a Methodist Episcopal Church. The *History of Tioga, Chemung, Tompkins and Schuyler Counties*, published in 1879, says the building was constructed in 1834 at a cost of $3,000 and seated 350 people. (Courtesy of the Groton Town Clerk's archives.)

The Free Church at Peruville was one of two churches in the hamlet of Peruville. No pictures have been located of that religious structure. This picture is of the Methodist Episcopal Church of Peruville, which was constructed in 1834 at a cost of $3,000. Notice the tall steeple built to hold a church bell.

This later view of the Methodist Episcopal Church of Peruville shows a steeple shorter than the one in the previous picture. The building was lost to fire in the late 1960s or early 1970s.

Four

HOUSES AROUND TOWN

Originally built in 1819 as the Baptist meetinghouse, the building was located farther south on Main Street. This early Greek Revival clapboard structure is two-and-a-half stories and was built by Ebenezer Williams, an early settler of Groton. Moved to its current location in 1843, it became the residence for the Harris family and is currently the museum for the Town of Groton Historical Association.

Currently the office of Ward and Murphy Attorneys at Law, this was a family home for many years. The fancy trim work still exists on this small house located on Main Street. The house partially visible to the left was razed to build a gasoline station. (Courtesy of Teresa Robinson.)

Once the home of Harry and Ione Masters, this house was located on Main Street. It was removed in the 1960s to make room for construction of the First National Bank of Groton. The sign in the window reads, "Dorethy's Beauty Salon." The salon was owned by Dorethy Pulling, aunt to the author of this publication. The car is a 1950 Buick. (Courtesy of the History Center in Tompkins County.)

This large, stately mansion is located on South Main Street. There was a time when it became apartments, but today it is a single-family home. The four Ionic columns dominate the main facade. (Courtesy of the Town of Groton Historical Association.)

Cortland St., looking West, Groton, N.Y.

This picture shows the home of Dr. Miles Goodyear on Cortland Street. Goodyear bequeathed funds for the construction of the Goodyear Memorial Library, as shown on page 23. In the 1950s, the building was used as the Kingdom Hall of Jehovah's Witnesses. That building was razed in the 1960s to construct a new place of worship. (Courtesy of the History Center in Tompkins County.)

The Reynolds Andrews residence is located on the southwest corner of Cortland and Church Streets. It became the home of Dr. Willard Short, with medical offices in the lower portion entering on the west end of the building. The Dutch Colonial–style home was built in 1895 by Robert Crandall Reynolds and features a gambrel roof and flared eaves. Notice the windows with decorative lead tracery.

The home of Welthea Marsh is located at 115 Williams Street. Actively interested in music, the Marsh family often sat on their porch and played instruments while citizens sat along the curb to listen. Shown are Welthea Backus Marsh standing to the right of the shrub; her mother, Sophia Mix Backus, sitting; Welthea's granddaughter Mary Tanner with the instrument; and Welthea's daughter Florence Lillian Marsh Tanner near the steps.

This stately brick house was the home of Jennie Conant Conger. Born in 1849 in Groton and educated at the Groton Academy, her husband, Frank Conger, was a business and financial head of the Groton Bridge Company and a buyer for the Conger family store. They were married in 1872. The home is located on William Street just north of the Marsh home and still exists today.

RESIDENCE OF E. P. WATROUS, GROTON, N.Y.

This early-1900s Verne Morton picture shows the home of Edgar P. Watrous, which is located on Park Street. At one time, the area in front of the home was all property of Watrous and was landscaped much like a park, hence the name of the street. Watrous was born on May 10, 1853, and died on August 10, 1939. This house is still a one-family residence today.

This photograph shows the houses on the south side of Elm Street. They look much like this today. The fourth house, 110 Elm Street, was the home of Robert and Ethel Booth. Booth was the director of the Booth Funeral Home, and his home served as the location of many funeral services. (Courtesy of the Town of Groton Historical Association.)

Located at 111 Sykes Street is this home that was once the home of Lionel Evans, and prior to that, it belonged to Cora Cook. The house stills looks like this today.

This was how the Village Memorial Park looked before the current swimming pool was added. Notice the lady sitting at the pond. The houses in the background are on the east side of Sykes Street and were built for housing employees of the Smith Corona Typewriter Company. Some of them have been removed since this picture was taken, but others still exist.

Located in Peruville and referred to as the Kratochvil house, Matthew Kratochvil purchased this house for $15,000 from Arthur Darling. No purchase date was indicated. Kratochvil's two sons tried farming but were unsuccessful and died in debt. Jake Kratochvil sold the property at an unknown date. The French Second Empire–style house includes a mansard roof, brackets, ornate trim, and dormer windows. (Courtesy of the Groton Town Clerk's archives.)

Located on Old Peruville Road is this beautiful home with a lovely wrap-around porch. Mary Adams lived here for many years and took pride in its care. It still looks much like this today. (Courtesy of the Town of Groton Historical Association.)

Located at 1 Sobers Road is this home with an American craftsman–style porch. It is a typical 19th-century farmhouse. The immediate area around this home is no longer used for farmland. The picture was taken in 1976. (Courtesy of the Groton Town Clerk's archives.)

In 1841, at the age of 12, John McKellar arrived from Scotland with his parents and siblings. McKellar married Amanda Halladay of West Groton in 1863 and built this house. Today this is a bed and breakfast and has been updated since this 1976 picture. Also existing today on the corner of Lick Street and County Road 107 is a house built in the same style by McKellar's older brother Archibald. (Courtesy of the Groton Town Clerk's archives.)

Located at 328 Salt Road, it is believed that this Italianate-style farmhouse was built about 1865. Notice the roof brackets and the small side porches. This 1976 picture shows the farm outbuildings. Tall, majestic trees shade the north side of the house. (Courtesy of the Town of Groton Clerk's archives.)

Located in the West Groton area, this house is on the site of a former barrel factory that was owned and operated by William Bulkley. Morris and Catherine Halladay owned this home at a later date. (Courtesy of Colleen Pierson.)

Isaac Allen, originally from Vermont, founded the settlement in the area of West Groton Corners about 1804. He built the first store, established a tavern, and was an extensive landowner in the vicinity. This 1976 picture shows the Isaac Allen house, built in 1820, which is located at 842 Cobb Street. (Courtesy of the Groton Town Clerk's archives.)

Built in 1824 as the Salt Road Tavern for Miles Riggs, this Federal-style structure is located on the southwest corner of Elm Street Extension and Salt Road. Upon completion, Riggs publicly announced that if a knot could be found in the wood of his new home, he would give the building to that person. No knot was found. Carved on the stone at the front entrance is 1824. (Courtesy of the Groton Town Clerk's archives.)

Abolitionist Rev. Marcus Harrison built this Federal Greek Revival transition-style parsonage in 1825 for his young wife, Ullily Amelia, to remind her of her southern home. Harrison was the pastor of the East Congregational Church, which stood on the northwest corner of Salt Road and New York State Route 222. Joseph Stickles purchased the house in 1876 and added a room on the north side with a porch. (Courtesy of the Groton Town Clerk's archives.)

Built on Salt Road for Amasa Barrows in 1825, this Cape Cod home has a large fireplace with a built-in bake oven, which is back-to-back with two other fireplaces that share one chimney. In 1870, Barrows's son Storrs planted evergreens as a health measure and to create a windbreak on the barren hilltop location. (Courtesy of the Groton Town Clerk's archives.)

It is believed this Greek Revival–style house at 226 Clark Street Extension was built around 1840. Over the front door is a diamond-faceted block with heavy beveled framing, which is typical of many Groton houses. (Courtesy of the Groton Town Clerk's archives.)

Located on New York State Route 222, this Greek Revival–style house has an Italianate-style addition. This 1976 picture shows eyebrow windows, brackets, and ornamental woodwork on the front porch. It was probably constructed is the 1870s. (Courtesy of the Groton Town Clerk's archives.)

This 1901 picture shows the Morton homestead that is located on Old Stage Road. Photographer Verne Morton and his brother Neal never married and lived together in this house, which had belonged to their parents, Porter and Dorothy Jane Smith Morton. The History Center in Tompkins County has Verne's original glass plates, and copies of pictures can be ordered from them. (Courtesy of Teresa Robinson.)

This Greek Revival–style home is located on New York State Route 38 north of the village. Originally called the Clapp farm, it was one of the best-known dairy farms of this area. It was sold to a James E. Ryan, who sold it to Ernest Childs in 1915, at which time Childs auctioned the farm animals and equipment. It was probably constructed in the 1880s. (Courtesy of the Groton Town Clerk's archives.)

Five

BUSINESSES
AND MANUFACTURING

The First National Bank of Groton has been a supporter of the community, including businesses and manufacturers, since 1865. The community bank, which still exists today, employs local people. This sketch is from a check dating back to 1901, showing the bank when it was located on the corner of Main and Mill Streets. Mill Street is now West Cortland Street.

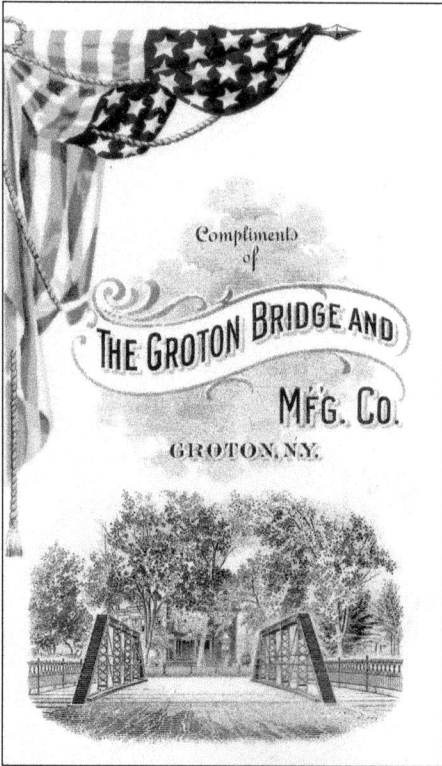

Compliments
of
THE GROTON BRIDGE AND
MFG. CO.
GROTON, N.Y.

The Charles Perrigo and Company was established by Charles and Lyman Perrigo as early as 1849 as a foundry and machine shop. In 1877, the firm began the manufacture of iron bridges. Soon afterward, the Groton Iron Bridge Company was formed and incorporated. In 1887, the Perrigo's company merged to become the Groton Bridge and Manufacturing Company. It is believed that this booklet may have been used by salesmen.

A group of employees from the Groton Bridge and Manufacturing Company are shown here. Since most appear to be dressed in business suits, these may be the salesmen for the company. (Courtesy of the Town of Groton Historical Association.)

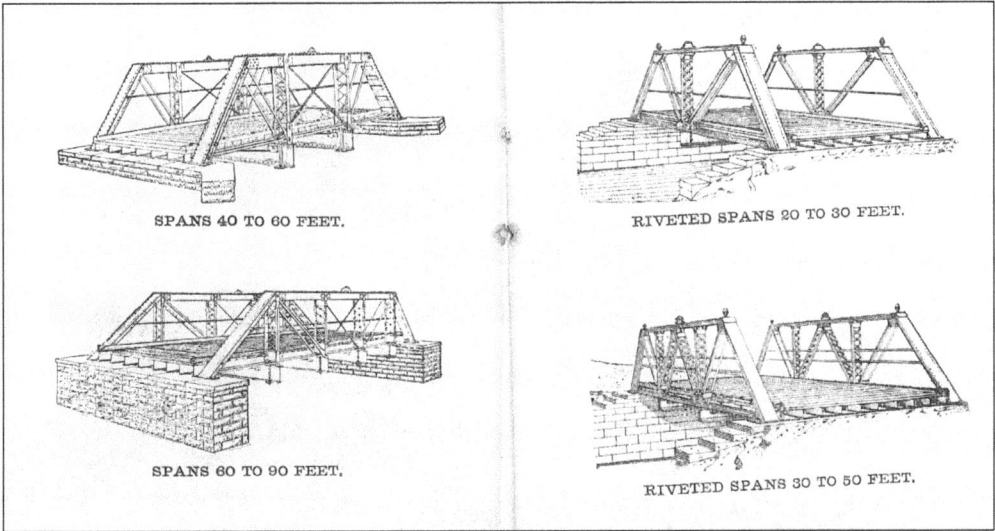

SPANS 40 TO 60 FEET.

RIVETED SPANS 20 TO 30 FEET.

SPANS 60 TO 90 FEET.

RIVETED SPANS 30 TO 50 FEET.

Shown here are some of the styles of bridges manufactured by the Groton Bridge and Manufacturing Company, as seen in the sales booklet of which the cover is shown on the previous page. Groton bridges were constructed throughout the United States and other countries. Today many Groton bridges are listed in a database of historic bridges in the United States of America, past and present.

Between late 1910 and 1912, Groton's Otto Petermann began designing the Standard Folding Typewriter No. 3. In 1911, the name of the machine is changed to Corona 3, and it was still described as a "Standard Folding Typewriter." The Corona 3, with a folding forward carriage and a three-bank keyboard, was launched in February 1912. A three-bank keyboard allowed three characters on each type bar.

This gentleman is demonstrating how to operate a road roller, which was manufactured by the Monarch Road Roller Company of Groton. The toolbox on the side displays the number 62. In 1913, the Monarch Road Roller Company had an order from the government for six machines. Four machines were to be shipped for use in the Philippines and two for paving contractors in Brazil.

MONARCH ROAD ROLLER CO., Groton, N. Y.

These buildings are the manufacturing locations of Monarch Road Roller Company. The company manufactured steamrollers, threshers, traction engines, and other heavy road machinery that was shipped by rail. When the doors closed in November 1917, some of the buildings were later incorporated into a honey-processing plant.

Harry Masters, left, was born in 1876. Listed in the 1910 and 1920 censuses as a farmer and a dealer in stock, or cattle, he was the owner of this business. The Donley sisters, Josephine and Catherine, had a hat shop on the second floor. They sold their business to M. L. Ford of Ludlowville by 1918. Looking closely, hats can be seen in the windows.

The Standard Typewriter Company is the wooden structure on the right. The large brick building on the left is the Groton Carriage Company. The street running between the two buildings is Spring Street. The Groton Carriage Company was organized as a stock company in 1876 and was known for its high grade of work, including buggies, spring wagons, surreys, and cutters.

This postcard was used to advertise and promote the Groton Carriage Company. Notice the company encouraged people to buy all four modes of transportation displayed here so that "you can go as you please."

While on a train in 1909, Benn Conger met a passenger who was operating a portable typewriter. Wanting to keep a typewriter business in Groton, Conger located the inventor and formed a corporation to buy the patent. In 1916, he built the factory shown here using the brick building of the former Groton Carriage Works. Employees could access the nearby gymnasium through the attached covered walkway.

This picture is of the First National Bank of Groton when it was located on the corner of Main and West Cortland Streets. As indicated on the second-floor windows, the law office of Myer Karp was located there, along with the General Insurance office. Today this building is occupied by Robert C. Dempsey Insurance.

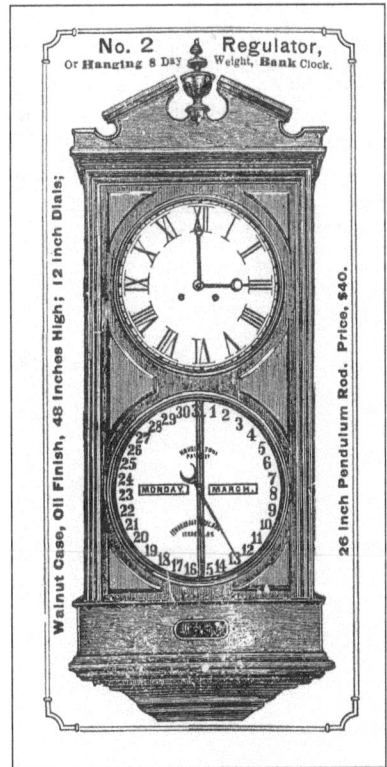

This advertisement shows a clock like the one seen in the bank picture on page 94. This No. 2 Regulator wall clock manufactured by Ithaca Clock Company dates back to at least 1875. The First National Bank of Groton began in May 1865, so it is possible it would have purchased a clock in 1875.

This interior view of the First National Bank of Groton shows Walter Gale on the left, Herbert Gleason standing on the far right, Ida Bacon seated at the desk, and John Hoff in the chair. It is believed that Frank Begent is the man wearing a hat and Henry Huff is standing in front of the safe. The wall clock can be seen in the lobby of today's bank building. (Courtesy of the Town of Groton Historical Association.)

This tall brick building on the east side of Main Street was the home of the post office. The post office later moved across the street to the building that is currently Main Street Pizzeria. A new facility was later built on the corner of Cayuga and Cortland Streets. The building shown in this picture exists today. (Courtesy of Teresa Robinson.)

The building on the left is the Groton Roller Flour Mill that was once owned by Jay G. Beach. It is located on the east side of Cayuga Street.

The Central Hotel, later known as the Tavern, was located on Main Street. The Corona Typewriter Company factory was built around this building. (Courtesy of Teresa Robinson.)

Here is Main Street showing Elm Street on the left going up the hill. A Gulf gasoline station is on the right, and the office of the *Journal and Courier* newspaper is to its left. Someone is inside the kiosk that sits in front of the newspaper building. Is this person selling newspapers? The car dealership on the far left is Peters' Ford.

This is the Main Street Garage. The building on the left with the porch houses Groton's American Legion today. (Courtesy of the Town of Groton Historical Association.)

The Sunnyside Greenhouses were located on Williams Street. An October 1926 article from Groton's *Journal and Courier* mentions that Clarence Howell was the proprietor of Sunnyside Greenhouses. Howell was born in September 1887 in Lansing.

Dunlap's was a furniture store located on the northwest corner of Cayuga and West Cortland Street. The building still exists today, but the two on the immediate right are no longer there. The two-story building shown farther down Cayuga Street is still in the same location, but the porches have been enclosed.

This Main Street picture shows the Grand Union's Super Ette store. To the left is the Groton Restaurant. Some buildings are no longer there, and others still exist with changes to the facades. (Courtesy of the Town of Groton Historical Association.)

The Harris 5¢ to $1 store was a longtime business in Groton once owned by Nelson Harris. The windows appear to be covered in preparation for changing the display. To the right is Bell Electric, a business once owned by Clayton Bell. Both these buildings exist today, but the 5¢ to $1 store is currently empty. The Bell Electric building now has apartments on the first and second floors.

This is another view of the Harris 5¢ to $1 store. It was a convenient place to shop for gifts, office supplies, school supplies, candy, and any other item a person would need. Having been a longtime asset to the Groton community, it is missed by many who remember it.

A winter scene of a grocery store shows people had fun with the deep snowbanks. A sign signifies "Pikes Peak" at the top of the snow bank on the right. Another sign reading, "Pull Me Out of Here" indicates someone placed shoes in the snowbank to make it look like someone was stuck. Located at 135 Main Street, today this building houses the Early Settler. (Courtesy of Teresa Robinson.)

A 1960s picture shows WCW Drycleaners on the west side of Main Street. Wilkins Castle was managed by Dorethy Pulling. The Western Auto is next door in the same building. The structure was lost to fire in the 1970s. This is where the Terry Graves Memorial Park is now located. The village electric truck hoists a man in the bucket to hang Christmas decorations across Main Street. (Courtesy of the Town of Groton Historical Association.)

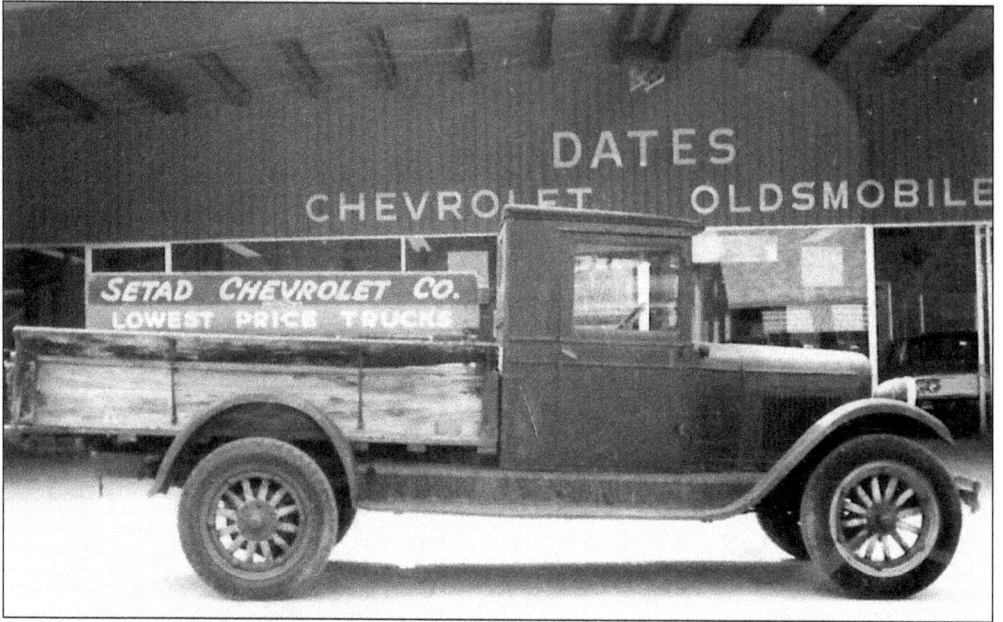

The truck shown in this picture was owned by businessman Karl Dates. The building for Dates Chevrolet is in the background. Notice the sign in the back of the truck, reading, "Setad Chevrolet Co. Lowest Price Trucks." Dates also owned a business in nearby Moravia. "Setad" is "Dates" spelled backwards. The Dates business in Groton later became Walters Chevrolet and is currently M and J Chevrolet.

Old-fashioned shopping days were once a popular way to hold summer sales. On the right is Ina McLear who co-owned the Jean Ann Shop with Dorothy Ostrander. This August 1963 picture shows McLear dressed for the occasion in old-fashioned styles. Although the person looking at clothing is unidentified, she could be Dorothy Ostrander. Currently Groton Hobby Shop, the building is located at 129 Main Street.

Six

PEOPLE

Born in Groton in 1840, Dexter Hubbard Marsh graduated from the Groton Academy in 1859. One of the cofounders of the First National Bank of Groton, Marsh was the bank's first clerk and became its president in 1890. While traveling in November 1895 on business to Chicago, Marsh was overcome with pneumonia and died there. He personally financed many large and small businesses in Groton. (Courtesy of the Groton Town Historian archives.)

Born 1841 in Groton, Welthea Backus married Dexter Marsh in 1862. Educated at the Groton Academy, she was the first and only woman bank president of the First National Bank of Groton and held that office from 1896 to 1901. Resigning in 1901 and then severely suffering for many months, Welthea died at her home in 1909. There were only three other woman bank presidents in New York State before her. (Courtesy of the Groton Town Historian archives.)

Corydon Conger was known to have one of the largest mercantile businesses on the Lehigh Valley Railroad between Pennsylvania and Auburn, New York. C. W. Conger and Company was established by him and his oldest son, Frank. Constructing its brick building in 1879, the business delivered merchandise door-to-door into the country. Conger was credited with the establishment of the Groton Carriage Works, the Groton Bridge Company, and the Crandall Typewriter Company.

Born in Groton in 1849 and educated at the Groton Academy, Frank Conger was known as the best businessman in Groton's early days. He was the head of the financial aspects of Groton Bridge Works and the buyer for C. W. Conger and Company. In a severe railroad wreck, he came upon a young child whose parents had died in the crash. He and his wife adopted two-year-old Oressa.

Benn Conger, son of Corydon and Mary Benoni Conger, was an entrepreneur and invested in many businesses in Groton. He served as president of the Corona Typewriter Company, as a New York State assemblyman (1900–1901), and as a New York State senator (1909–1910).

Born in 1854 and educated at the Groton Academy, Jay Conger, the youngest son of Corydon and Mary Benoni Conger, married Florence Hathaway in 1878. Jay was a cashier at the First National Bank of Groton from 1901 to 1902 and became its president for nine years beginning in 1902.

Doctor and Mary Conant Tarbell lived in the Peruville area. Born in 1834 and given the first name of Doctor, he is shown in his Civil War uniform. He joined the 32nd New York Infantry in 1862 and was a commissary in the Army of the Potomac. He was a prisoner of war from 1864 to 1865. Mary was raised by the Sylvanus Larned family in Peruville and married Doctor in May 1865.

Born in Groton in 1831, Sylvester Pennoyer became one of the most earnest men to be named in the connection with the early history of Oregon. Having completed his Harvard College education in 1854, he left his boyhood home of Groton and moved to Oregon, taught in public schools, became involved in the lumber business, and was editor of a newspaper. In 1886, he was elected governor of Oregon. (Courtesy of Paul Duden.)

The note on the postcard identifies this mailman as A. E. Fish. The 1910 census indicates that Alexander E. Fish was a rural delivery mailman and lived on South Main Street in Groton. He is listed in the 1920 census as A. Eleck Fish, age 60. The carriage may be one manufactured by the Groton Carriage Company.

This early-1900s picture shows a group of men at the corner of West South Street and Peru Road. The man with the mustache sitting in the cutter is Otto Peterman. The cutter could be one manufactured by the Groton Carriage Company. The house in the background still exists.

This 1911 photograph taken by Verne Morton is of John Bradt, who seems to be very proud of his bicycle. Could it be new? In the background is the Morton family home on Old Stage Road. (Courtesy of The History Center in Tompkins County.)

Porter Morton, born in 1845, was Verne's father. The Morton homestead is shown on page 86. Porter, a farmer for many years, inherited a share in a carriage and wagon business, which supplemented his income. (Courtesy of the History Center in Tompkins County.)

Dorothy Jane Smith married Porter Morton, and together they had four children, of which only two grew to adulthood. Dorothy and Porter were the third generation of Mortons to raise a family on the Morton homestead. (Courtesy of the History Center in Tompkins County.)

Born in Groton in 1868, Verne Morton became a photographer and produced 12,000 photographs. He was one of four children, but only he and his brother Neil survived to adulthood. The collection of his original glass plates is at the History Center in Tompkins County. (Courtesy of the History Center in Tompkins County.)

Mary Stickles was the granddaughter of John and Amada Halladay McKellar. The McKellar home is shown on page 81. (Courtesy of the Groton Town Historian archives.)

This is the Betts family. Shown in this 1906 picture is John and Lillian Betts with their daughters Frances and Laura. The oldest, Frances, is kneeling. (Courtesy of the Groton Town Historian archives.)

This is a later picture of John and Lillian Betts. (Courtesy of the Groton Town Historian archives.)

When looking at individual pictures of young people at different ages, it is interesting to see the fashions, how they posed, and their hairstyles. Shown here is Edith M. Voorhees, born about 1903, the daughter of J. Overton and Louise M. Voorhees. The picture could have been taken at the time she graduated from high school.

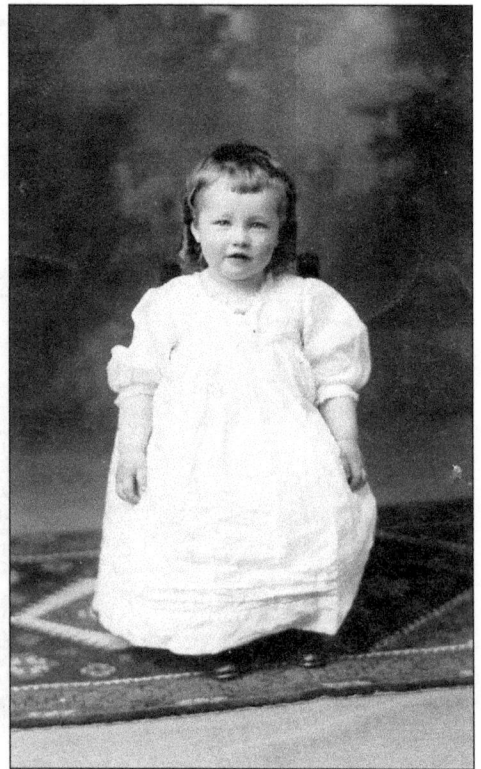

This delightful child is Paul Voorhees, son of J. Overton and Louise M. Voorhees. The note on the back of the 1909 photograph indicates he is 23 months old, and says, "I haven't a girl to send you to look at, this is my youngest boy." The card was sent to someone at the Cortland Hospital who just had a baby girl. Paul was born about 1907.

Dr. G. M. Gilchrist, with his horse and wagon, stops at the Morton homestead so that Verne Morton can take his picture. (Courtesy of the History Center in Tompkins County.)

Dr. G. M. Gilchrist can make his house calls much quicker in his new car. This 1913 photograph shows him with a small child on his lap. (Courtesy of the History Center in Tompkins County.)

Shown in this picture is a group of World War I noncommissioned and commissioned officers. The picture was taken in front of the World War I board of veterans' names, which was located on Main Street. The building in the background is the Groton High School, which fronted on Church Street. Although names of those in the picture are too numerous to mention, they are identified by the town of Groton historian.

Shown on the left in this picture is one of Groton's barbers, John Clark. His barbershop is shown behind him. The other person is not identified. (Courtesy of Teresa Clark Robison.)

Mary Morris Clark is dressed very nicely to show off her new baby, James. Mary was the wife of the barber shown in the previous picture. (Courtesy of Teresa Clark Robinson.)

This picture shows Albert VanBuskirk with his wife, Rose Hopkins VanBuskirk, to his right. The other ladies are Emily Hopkins and Mame Chapman. Albert was born about 1868 and married Rose about 1890. She was born about 1871. He was a machinist at a typewriter company in Groton. Are they dressed in costume for a play or is it the style of their ancestors? (Courtesy of the Groton Town Historian archives.)

Ione Downing was born on May 16, 1884, and this picture was taken in honor of her 12th birthday. She was the daughter of Marshall and Mary Downing. She married Harry M. Masters on October 14, 1906. Pictures of Masters's business and their Main Street home are shown earlier in this book.

Charles V. Coggshall was born in November 1877 and lived about two miles north of the village on New York State Route 38. He owned and operated an apple cider mill. He died in October 1969 one month before he was 92 years old. His former home is currently owned by the Michael Smith family, and his apple cider building is now Sarge's Auction House. (Courtesy of the Groton Town Historian archives.)

Cora Coggshall was born about 1876, the daughter of VanBuren and Catherine Coggshall. She is a sister of Charles, shown in the previous picture. The 1920 census lists her as living in Locke on Groton State Road. Her mother was living with her at that time. (Courtesy of the Groton Town Historian archives.)

This picture shows the members of the 1958–1959 Groton Women's Bowling Association. Those working at the Smith Corona Typewriter Company factory bowled at the nearby Smith Corona Club located on the northwest corner of Main and Spring Streets. The identities of the people pictured here can be found at the Groton Town Historian's office or the Town of Groton Historical Association. (Courtesy of the Town of Groton Historical Association.)

Cora Cook once lived on Sykes Street in a house shown on page 79. (Courtesy of the Groton Town Historian archives.)

Dorethy Mae Palmer, daughter of Elmer and Florence Soper Palmer, was a beautician whose shop was located in the home of Harry and Ione Masters. She later was the manager of WCW Drycleaners. She and her husband, Mark Pulling, lived in Groton for many years, retiring and relocating to Florida in 1966.

The village of Groton celebrated its centennial in 1960. The centennial committee from left to right includes (first row) George Gavras, Robert Dempsey, Gerald Moses, Thomas Heffron, and Robert Share; (second row) Ed Trinkle, Ruth Maricle, Myrtle Gallow, Jo Walpole, Elsie Thompson, and Earl Metzgar; (third row) Searle Moon, Harold Lily, Steve Lucas, Elwin Baird, and Art Walpole. Committee members not in the picture are Gerald Barry and Irving Henry. (Courtesy of the Town of Groton Historical Association.)

During the 1960 centennial celebration for the village of Groton, a parade was held, and many people came out to watch. Nine-year old April Lane was from neighboring Cayuga County. Dressed in her 1860s fashion and pushing an antique doll carriage, she grew up to become Groton's town clerk. (Courtesy of the Town of Groton Historical Association.)

Shown in the parade for the 1960 centennial celebration for the village of Groton is Sheldon Clark, driving the tractor traveling east on Cortland Street. Harold Scheffler, Groton School's agriculture teacher and adviser to Groton's Future Farmers of America, rides on the wagon. (Courtesy of the Town of Groton Historical Association.)

Steve Lucas was 68 at the time this picture was taken in 1983. He was a builder by profession and constructed the clubhouse at Groton's Stonehedges Golf Course. He was also active as a member of the Groton American Legion and the village of Groton's 1960 centennial committee. He and his wife, Freda, built their home on Locke Road. (Courtesy of Freda Lucas.)

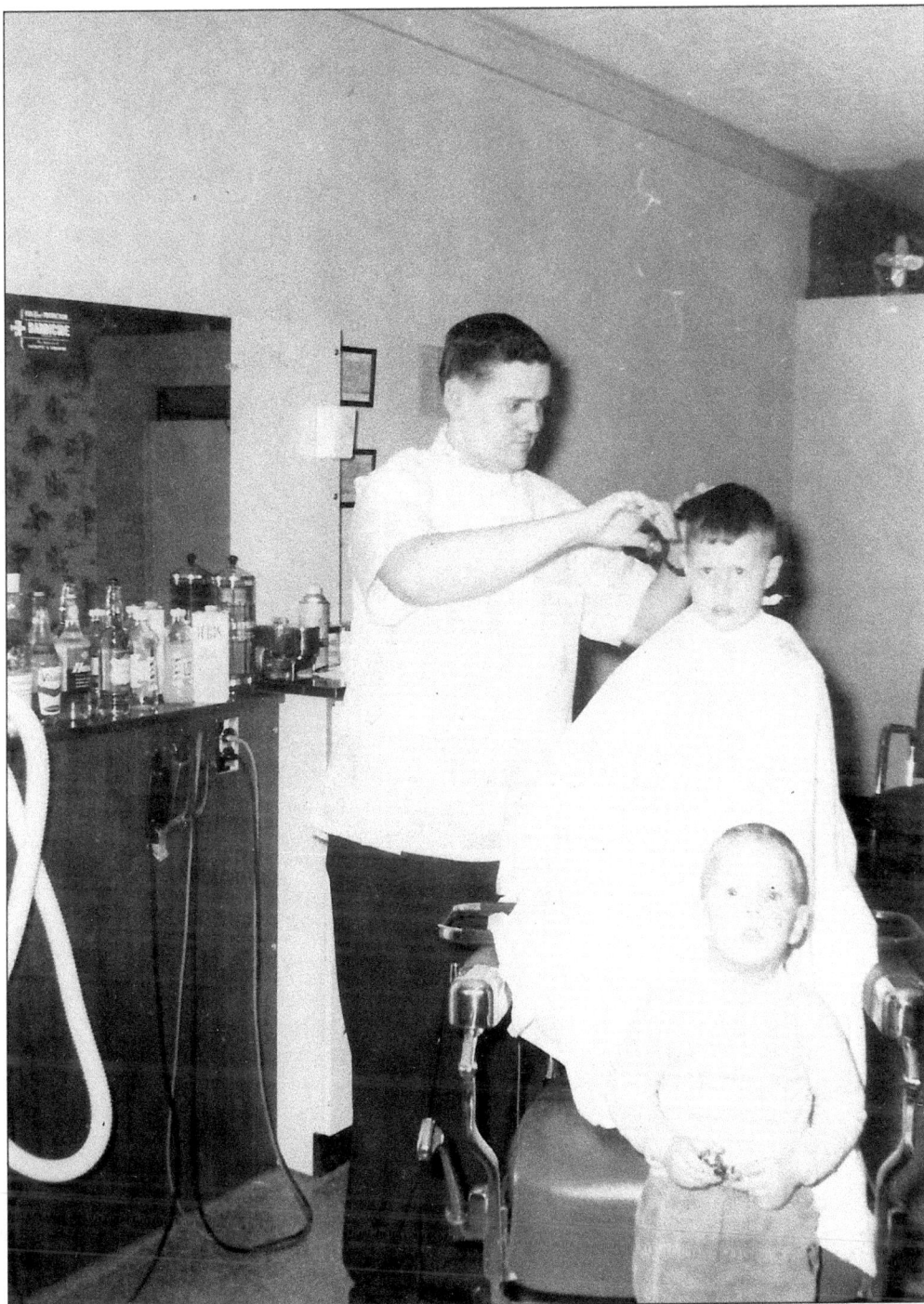

This 1966 picture shows Groton barber Frank Satterly cutting the hair of his oldest son, Mark. Waiting patiently is younger son, Eric. Frank had also been the mayor of the village of Groton for eight years. He became the director of Public Works and Utilities for the village from 1981 to 2000. A pedestrian bridge crossing Owasco Creek in Groton was built to honor Frank. (Courtesy of the Town of Groton Historical Association.)

LaVena and Richard Court taught at Groton School from 1962 until their retirements in 1982. Well known and respected by students, he coached boys' sports, becoming the athletic director in 1971. Following his death in 1996, the high school gymnasium was named for him. LaVena taught New York State and American history. She now lives in Marathon and has been active with the historical society there and in Groton. (Courtesy of LaVena Court.)

Leslie C. Graves was the superintendent of schools in Groton from 1963 until his retirement in 1983. Instrumental in overseeing changes in sports at Groton School, he was a driving force behind the formation of the Interscholastic Athletic Conference and was inducted into the Groton Sports Hall of Fame in 2003. He and his wife, Marge, raised three children, Terrence, Eric, and Kathy. Terrence was killed in Vietnam in February 1968. (Courtesy of LaVena Court.)

Dedicated in 2001 by those in the community, the Terrence Graves Memorial is located on Main Street. This monument recognizes the lieutenant and notes that he posthumously received the Medal of Honor. Since space is too limited here to mention the many veterans from the Groton area, the author thanks them for their dedicated times of service, especially those who gave the ultimate sacrifice. (Courtesy of Debbie Hubbard.)

BIBLIOGRAPHY

American Agriculturist Farm Directory of Yates, Schuyler, Tompkins and Seneca Counties New York. New York: Orange Judd Company, 1914.

Corth, Richard, Lynn Cunningham Truame, Carol Kammen, and Fred Muratori. *The Architectural Heritage of Tompkins County.* Ithaca, NY: DeWitt Historical Society, 2002.

Court, LaVena. *A Salute to Groton's Heritage.* Groton: Town of Groton Historical Association, 1976.

DeWitt Historical Society of Tompkins County. *Images of Rural Life: Photographs of Verne Morton.* Ithaca, NY: DeWitt Historical Society, 1984.

Dieckmann, Jane Marsh. *A Short History of Tompkins County.* Ithaca, NY: DeWitt Historical Society, 1986.

Dieckmann, Jane Marsh, ed., with other contributors. *The Towns of Tompkins County: From Podunk to the Magnetic Springs.* Ithaca, NY: DeWitt Historical Society, 1998.

French, J. H. *Historical and Statistical Gazetteer of New York State.* Interlaken, NY: Reprinted by Heart of the Lakes Publishing, 1986. Originally published in 1860 by R. P. Smith, Syracuse, NY.

Historic Preservation in Tompkins County. Ithaca, NY: Tompkins County Department of Planning, December 1977 (second printing).

Historical Souvenir of Groton, N.Y. Albany, NY: "Grips" Valley Gazette Historical Souvenir Series No. 6, October 1899.

Kammen, Carol, ed., with other contributors. Ithaca, NY: *Place Names of Tompkins County.* Office of the Tompkins County Historian, 2004.

Visit us at
arcadiapublishing.com